WILDLIFE AT RISK

WOLVES

Gillian Standring

WILDLIFE AT RISK

Bears
Birds of Prey
Elephants
Gorillas
Monkeys
Pandas
Rhinos
Seals and Sea Lions
Tigers
Turtles and Tortoises
Whales and Dolphins
Wolves

Cover: These wolves live in a wildlife reserve so are safe from human hunters.

Series designer: Marilyn Clay
Book editors: Sue Hadden and
  Joan Walters

First published in 1991 by
Wayland (Publishers) Ltd
61 Western Road, Hove
East Sussex BN3 1JD, England

**British Library Cataloguing in
Publication Data**
Standring, Gillian
  Wolves.–(Wildlife at risk)
  I. Title   II. Series
  599.74

  ISBN 0-7502-0147-9

Typeset by Dorchester Typesetting Group Ltd.
Printed and bound in Italy by L.E.G.O. S.p.A.

Contents

All words printed in **bold** are explained
in the glossary on page 30.

WOLVES AND THEIR RELATIVES

You can easily recognize a wolf as a member of the dog family. It looks like an Alsatian (or German Shepherd dog) with its long, strong legs, sharp nose and ears and wide mouth full of pointed teeth. Wolves' closest relatives are probably the huskies of Alaska, northern Canada and Greenland. These tough **domesticated** cousins have been bred to pull heavy loads across snow and ice. They are found in areas where some wild wolves still live.

A fully-grown wolf is the largest and strongest wild dog in the world.

Inuit sled-dogs, though domesticated, look and behave much like their wild relatives.

Other wild dogs live and hunt in groups, just like wolves. They are found in many parts of the world. In southern Africa there are hunting dogs, each one with its own pattern of brown, yellow and white patches. The Indian dhole looks like a small wolf. South American forests and **pampas** are the home of short-legged but fierce bush dogs.

Not all wild dogs live in large groups. Jackals of Africa and Asia live in pairs or small family groups, and so do North American coyotes. The long-legged maned wolf of South America prefers to live alone, like its relatives the foxes. Arctic foxes live in the very cold northern part of the world. Bat-eared and kit foxes and the tiny fennec fox all live in deserts, where daytime temperatures are very hot.

Facts about the wolf

Scientific name: *Canis lupus*

Length of head and body: 100-150 cm.

Length of tail: 30-50 cm.

Weight: 20-80 kg.
(Males are bigger than females.)

Number in litter: 4-7 (usually 5).

Age (in wild): 8-16 years.
(in captivity): up to 20 years.

Dingos are wild dogs of the Australian outback. They usually hunt alone, so this is probably a family group.

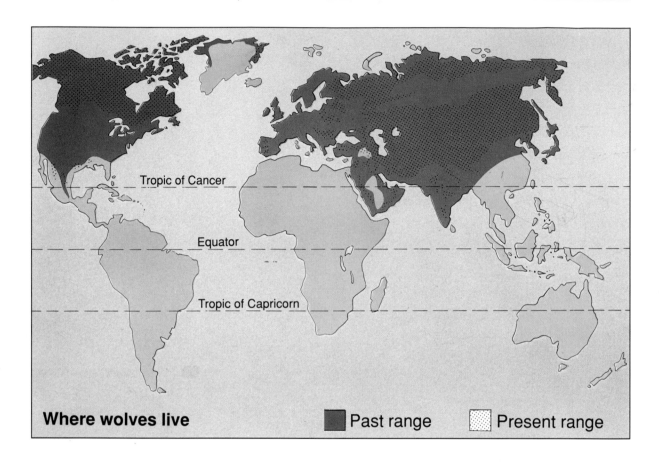

Where wolves live | Past range | Present range

In the past, wolves lived in more parts of the world than any other **mammals** except humans. This is no longer true and very few people are lucky enough to see wild wolves.

The map shows the parts of the world where wolves could be found in the past, and where they still survive today. There were once at least thirty different **subspecies** of wolf. Most have become **extinct**; only five or six subspecies survive today. A few wolves still live in Spain, Italy, Germany, eastern Europe, India and the Middle East. The last British wolves survived in Ireland and Scotland into the eighteenth century, but wolves were wiped out in England and Wales by about 1500. Nobody knows how many wolves live in the USSR and China.

Most wolves in North America are to be found in Alaska and Canada. In the American states of Texas and Louisiana, the unusual red wolf can only be found in tiny numbers.

Wolves are usually shy animals and it is extremely difficult to study them closely in the wild. Some scientists have used planes and helicopters to track wolves from the air, but most of our knowledge comes from hunters. They tell us that wolves are now almost impossible to find.

A tundra wolf goes hunting for small mammals and birds on the Alaskan tundra in summer.

As wolves live in so many different parts of the world, it is not surprising that they are not all exactly alike. Wolves vary a lot in size, colour and coat thickness. A wolf expert can tell at a glance which part of the world a wolf comes from.

The red wolf of Texas, which looks very like the grey wolf, is thought to be on the brink of extinction.

The biggest wolves with the thickest coats live in the far north. They hunt moose and caribou in the pine forests and snowy **tundra** of the Canadian and Russian Arctic. They are called tundra or timber wolves. Their coats are often very light in colour or almost white.

The thick, pale grey coat of the timber wolf keeps it warm and dry and helps to camouflage it when it hunts in the snow.

European wolves often take refuge deep in the forests where they can hide from farmers and hunters.

The wolves that still survive in Europe and central Asia are smaller and have greyish coats, sometimes almost black. They have become used to living quite close to human villages and farms. These wolves mainly feed on deer and small antelopes.

The smallest wolves come from the Middle East and India. They often have reddish or fawn fur and seem to live mainly alone or in small groups. This may be because they usually have to feed on smaller animals like rabbits and **rodents**. Their hunting grounds are often wide areas of dry grassland, scrub or semi-desert.

This wolf from Israel has a thin smooth coat, making it look smaller than the wolves from northern Europe.

LIFE IN THE WOLF PACK

Wolves are **sociable** animals that live together in groups called packs. A pack may contain from two to twenty-five wolves, all related to one another. They live and hunt within their own **territory**. Larger packs than this are very unusual. The size of a pack depends on space and food. Where wolves have plenty of space and lots of large animals to hunt, the packs will be large. Sometimes, in a very hard winter or a poor summer, when food is hard to find, large packs will split up for a time into smaller groups of two or three wolves.

In a wolf pack there are males and females of all ages. Each wolf must learn its position in the group.

The wolf family

Grey wolf	N. America Europe, Asia	Foxes	N. America, Europe, Asia
Red wolf	South-east USA	S. American foxes	S. America
Maned wolf	S. America	Arctic fox	Arctic regions
Dingo	New Guinea, Australia	Bat-eared fox	Southern Africa
Domestic dog	Worldwide	Coyote	N. America
Raccoon dog	Eastern Asia	Jackals	Africa, Asia
African hunting dog	Southern Africa	Dhole	India, Southeast Asia
Bush dog	S. America	Fennec	Sahara Desert

By living together in packs, wolves can defend their territories and food supply from other wolf packs. Together wolves can hunt and kill large animals such as moose and elk, which are too big for a single wolf to tackle. They can also share in caring for the young cubs. In the pack each wolf lives peacefully with the others, sharing its food and shelter, even when times are hard.

Wolves help each other to catch and kill their prey and then share the meal together.

Animals that live together in a group, like a wolf pack, need to be able to talk to each other. Wolves can tell each other many things by special signs. One wolf can find out the age of another wolf and whether it is male or female. It soon learns whether the other wolf wants to play, hunt, fight or just be alone.

Above This wolf's snarling face gives humans, as well as other wolves, a clear message, do not come any closer.

In a friendly tussle, the lower wolf rolls on its back to show that it gives in.

The way a wolf stands and holds its head and tail are clear signs seen at a distance. Are its ears pricked up or pressed back? Are its eyes wide open, its mouth grinning or all the teeth showing with the lips drawn back? Is its fur lying flat or standing on end? All these are signals to other wolves close by.

Wolves talk to each other when far apart by howling and barking. Each wolf has its own voice, which is recognized by all the others in the pack. When friendly wolves meet, they greet each other with yaps and squeaks. They rub together and sniff each other.

Like all dogs, wolves use their sharp sense of smell to pick up scent signals. They regularly mark their trails by spraying **urine** on bushes and rocks. The spray marks carry detailed messages about the age, sex and size of each wolf and how long ago it passed by. Strange wolves smell these messages and are warned away.

Two young European wolves raise their voices in a howl to show that they are members of the pack.

THE WOLF GOES HUNTING

From a rocky look-out a wolf searches its territory for the sight or smell of possible prey before it goes hunting.

The wolf is a very well-equipped hunter, with its strong jaws and sharp teeth. Its long, strong legs and big feet carry it far without tiring. Its hearing and sense of smell are very sharp. It can see better in dim light than we can.

A single wolf can often catch small animals for itself by pouncing, rather like a cat. But several wolves hunting together as a team can do even better. Late in the evening, wolves call to one another by howling. This gathers the pack animals from wherever they have spent the day and gets them in the mood for hunting.

An older, experienced wolf leads the pack in single file along a familiar trail. When they pick up the scent of an animal (often a deer) the wolves follow it, with noses to the ground. By moving in quickly from the right direction, **upwind**, the wolves get quite close before the deer knows they are there. When the deer begins to run, the wolves may spread out. Younger, faster animals move round to block the deer's path.

Some wolves drop back to rest while others take the lead. The chase goes on until the **prey** gets tired and begins to slow down. Then the whole pack closes in for the kill.

Above *A well-organized pack eagerly sets out on a hunting expedition.*

Left *At the end of a successful hunt a white-tailed deer provides plenty of food.*

BRINGING UP THE CUBS

In most wolf packs, only one pair **mate** and produce cubs each year. These are the top male and female wolves. They often stay together for life.

The **breeding season** is in early spring and the cubs are born two months later, in April or May. There are usually four to seven cubs in a **litter**. The other wolves may help the mother to dig a den in a bank. Here the cubs are born. At first they are blind and deaf. Their mother stays with them all the time, feeding them on her milk and keeping them warm.

These day-old wolf cubs, covered in short black fur, are completely helpless.

Breeding male and female wolves greet each other as partners by sniffing and licking.

All the wolves in the pack help to look after the litter. The cubs can see and hear at about two weeks old. Now their mother may leave them to go hunting with the pack. An 'auntie' stays to guard the cubs. When the others return, the cubs lick and bite at their **muzzles**. This makes the older wolves cough up pieces of meat. Young cubs eat partly **digested** meat, rather like baby food.

When they are old enough to be left alone, wolf cubs enjoy playing with old bones but stay close to the entrance of the den for safety.

When they are about five weeks old, the cubs begin to play at the den's entrance. They chase one another and pretend to fight. Each learns its position among the members of the pack and keeps this rank as it grows up.

WHY ARE WOLVES AT RISK?

A crowded world

To live and breed successfully, wolves need lots of room. Each pack may spend most of the time in its own territory but they do move about, in and out of other packs' areas. Wolves that have only small areas to live in are always in great danger of dying out.

When wolves have plenty of space and are left alone to hunt their natural prey they can lead peaceful and well-ordered lives. Only small wild areas are left for these European wolves.

Living and extinct wolves

Living subspecies	Extinct subspecies
Common European or grey wolf	Japanese wolf
Asian or Iranian wolf	Great Plains wolf
Tibetan or steppe wolf	Texas grey wolf
Eastern timber wolf	Newfoundland wolf
Tundra or northern wolf	Rocky Mountain wolf
Chinese wolf	Cascade Mountains wolf

Most wolves survive in parts of the world where there are still large undisturbed areas of forest, tundra, grassland or scrub. As we humans need more and more room, we leave less and less living space for wolves. In the busy and crowded countries of Europe, only small wild areas remain. In Britain and Scandinavia, humans have taken over most of the land for farming, forestry, factories or housing. They leave no room for wolves.

In Alaska, Canada and the USSR, where very few people live, there are still wild, open areas. Here, wolves go on living more or less naturally. But even in these areas they need protection by international laws. In other crowded countries such as India, China and Japan, most wolves have disappeared. They are allowed to survive only in places which no one wants for farms, villages or towns.

This North American forest was once wolf territory. Now the work of the logging industry has scared the wolves away.

Danger from people

Wolves and humans have shared their world for thousands of years. Long ago, when people lived in caves and simple shelters in the forests, wolves lived close by. They picked up bones and scraps of meat left by the human hunters. The wolves played a useful part as **scavengers**. In time, the humans and the wolves grew less afraid of each other. They may even have helped each other to hunt. Human babies and wolf cubs probably grew up together. Perhaps wolves were friendly with people just as our pet dogs are today.

The famous statue of a she-wolf feeding the twin babies Romulus and Remus, who later founded the city of Rome.

A frightening scene from early American pioneer days, showing starving wolves attacking a family of settlers.

Later, humans built houses and cities and grew their food by farming and keeping herds of animals. Sadly, they forgot that they had once lived peacefully alongside wolves. They began to think of wolves as fierce, dangerous killers of their farm animals and even of people. All sorts of stories were made up about wicked wolves, such as Little Red Riding Hood, the Three Little Pigs and the Seven Little Goats. Wolves were said to prowl the forests, terrifying people with their night-time howls, glowing red eyes and great fangs. In the end, most people believed the stories and forgot the truth about wolves.

Shooting animals that eat a farmer's crops or kill his stock is not only sport for the hunter but also provides him with valuable meat and furs to sell.

People turn land into farms to grow food crops for themselves and their domestic animals. But wild animals like deer, rabbits, mice and geese like to eat the crops. So farmers try to get rid of these animals. All these wild animals are the natural prey of wolves, but when they disappear from farmland, the wolves turn to hunting farm animals. In Spain and Italy, wolves kill hundreds of sheep and goats each year. The owners of the flocks protect their animals by killing as many wolves as possible.

After all, the farmers make their living by producing food for other people. This makes it hard for farmers and wolves to live together.

Wolves are also killed because they eat wild **game** animals that human hunters like to shoot for sport. In some places, the hunters pay a lot of money to shoot game and local people are glad for them to do so.

There are other reasons for killing wolves. Their **pelts** are sold to tourists and to make fur coats. Their heads make fine hunting **trophies**. Scientists study wolves' bodies to find out more about them. To the human hunters, money is more important than the future of a wild animal.

Was this wolf shot just for a hunting trophy?

Kill the beast!

For thousands of years, North American Indians and **Inuit** have killed wolves for their skins and as part of their ceremonies. They only killed small numbers, and to them wolves were an important part of the living world. Unfortunately there are other people who kill wolves only out of hatred and fear. They think that wolves are evil, or call them cowardly for killing defenceless deer. Some people believe wolves should be wiped out completely.

Sioux Indians hunting bison. They hid beneath wolf skins to get close to the bison.

In the USA, some sheep farmers use light aircraft to hunt wolves and other predators.

These people have used many horrible ways to try to get rid of wolves. They shoot them from helicopters, hunt them from horseback with packs of dogs, and chase them in trucks to exhaustion. They use poison baits which kill not only wolves but also other **predators,** such as foxes, raccoons, polecats, hawks and eagles.

Wolves all over the world have been destroyed in their thousands in the past, and sadly this still goes on. Recently, in central Scandinavia, the first wolves were seen south of the Arctic Circle for almost a hundred years. But one by one, the wolves were killed by local people who did not want to live so close to the wild animals. People who understand wolves know that humans have nothing to fear from them.

Cruel leg traps, set to catch large animals, often kill smaller creatures, like this polecat.

SAVING THE WOLF

As we have seen, there are still quite a lot of wolves in the more remote parts of North America, Europe and Asia. They survive well here if left in peace. But when wolves come too close to people, they are unwelcome. Sometimes professional hunters must kill some to control their numbers, but we need not wipe them out.

If wolves must be killed to control their numbers, or for any other reason, it should be done cleanly and painlessly by expert hunters who carefully choose which animals to shoot.

The Arctic tundra in summer has plenty of small mammals and birds and space, so it is a perfect hunting-ground for wolves.

To survive, wolves need large, undisturbed areas in wildlife **reserves** and national parks. Here both wolves and their prey are strictly protected from human hunters. This is already done in Canada and the USA, and on a smaller scale in Europe.

Some people, including scientists, would like some wolves born in zoos to be taken back to the wild. The animals can be set free in places where they once lived. This can be done only after very careful planning and with specially chosen animals. In Sweden, such a plan failed because the zoo-bred wolves could not look after themselves in the wild. Wolves have been successfully put back into one or two reserves in the USA, but it is very unlikely that they will ever again be important in European wildlife.

These wolves live in safety in a German national park.

The wolf is one of the world's great wild hunters. If it is still to exist in 100 years, or even in fifty, we must try to understand this animal better. How can we protect wolves if most people still think they are dangerous and unnecessary animals?

We need stricter laws to protect wolves. The Convention on Conservation of European Wildlife is an international law passed at Berne, Switzerland, in 1979. The law was signed by all the European countries where wolves live. Yet when fifteen wolves were killed in Scandinavia in the 1980s, no one was punished. In parts of North America, hunters who kill wolves for **bounty** are still thought of as heroes.

The only way to stop this is to tell more people the truth about wolves. In Minnesota, USA, an International Wolf Centre is being set up. Visitors can watch **captive** wolves and see displays that explain how wolves live. For most of us, our best chance of seeing wolves will be in zoos and wildlife parks. Here they are well cared for. Soon people may even be able to go on wolf-watching holidays. As more people come to love and understand wolves, these marvellous animals may face a brighter future.

Even in over-crowded parts of the world we should find some room for wolves to go on living side-by-side with humans.

Glossary

Bounty   A reward for catching or killing certain animals thought to be a nuisance.

Breeding season   The time of year when male and female animals mate.

Captive   Kept by humans in an enclosure.

Digested   Food that is broken down inside the body, so that the animal can take in its goodness.

Domesticated   Tamed and controlled by humans.

Extinct   No longer living anywhere on Earth.

Game   Wild animals hunted and killed by humans for sport and food.

Inuit   An Eskimo word that means 'the people'. This is the name that Eskimos prefer to be called.

Litter   The number of young produced at one time.

Mammals   Warm-blooded animals, with hair or fur, that feed their young on milk.

Mate   To come together as a male and a female to mate.

Muzzle   The mouth of a dog or a wolf.

Pampas   A large treeless plain in South America.

Pelt   The skin and fur of a mammal.

Predator   An animal that hunts and eats other animals.

Prey   An animal that is killed by another animal for food.

Reserve   A protected area in which animals can live in safety.

Rodent   A mammal with sharp, gnawing teeth. Rats and squirrels are rodents.

Scavenger   An animal which feeds off the remains of dead animals.

Sociable   An animal that likes to live with others of its kind.

Subspecies   A slightly different race of a particular species of animal. For example, some wolf subspecies are paler in colour.

Territory   An area of land where an animal normally lives, hunts and breeds.

Trophy   An animal's head that is put on display to show other people that it was killed by a hunter.

Tundra   The open, treeless landscape of Arctic areas. The soil deep in the ground is permanently frozen.

Upwind   Against the wind. When a wolf is upwind of a deer, the deer cannot smell the wolf.

Urine   The pale yellow liquid that is passed out of an animal's body some time after it has drunk water.

Further reading

Amazing Wolves and Wild Dogs   M. Ling (Dorling Kindersley, 1991)
Wolf Pack: tracking wolves in the Wild   Sylvia Johnson (Lerner USA, 1985)
Wolves   Candace Savage (Robert Hale, 1988)

Useful addresses

If you would like to help protect wolves, and other rare animals of the world, you might like to join one of these wildlife charities:

Fauna and Flora Preservation Society
79/83 North Street
Brighton
East Sussex BN1 1ZA

World Wide Fund for Nature
(Australia)
Level 7, St Martin's Tower
31 Market Street
GPO Box 528
Sydney NSW

World Wide Fund for Nature
(International)
Avenue du Mont Blanc
CH 1196 Gland
Switzerland

World Wide Fund for Nature
(UK)
Panda House
Weyside Park
Godalming
Surrey GU7 1XR

Picture acknowledgements
The photographs in this book were supplied by: Bruce Coleman Ltd cover (A. J. Purcell), 7, 15 right (E. + P. Bauer), 24 bottom (N. Devore), 29 (J. Foott), 12 right, 15 top, 16 bottom (U. Hirsch), 4, 8 (S. J. Kraseman), 7 (C. Ott), 5, 9 right, 22 (H. Reinhard), 4 (N. Rosing), 26 (L. Rue jnr), 27 (J. Shaw), 10 (G. Ziesler); Mary Evans 24 top; Hutchison 14 (V. & A. Wilkinson); Frank Lane Picture Agency 13 (C. Dani & I. Jeske), 17 (L. Lee Rue); Peter Newark's Western Americana 21; Oxford Scientific Films 11, 12 left, 18 (Animals Animals), 9 left (E. Bartov), 19 (Earth Scenes), 28 (P. Henry), 25 (M. Wendler); Survival Anglia 23 (Bomford & Barkowski), 16 (R. & J. Kemp); Topham 20 (G. Wright). The map on page 6 was drawn by John Yates.

Index